MATUR SNOW

MAYOR SNOW

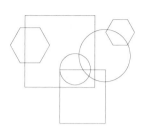

NICK THRAN

NIGHTWOOD EDITIONS

2015

Nightwood Editions
P.O. Box 1779
Gibsons, BC VON 1VO
Canada
www.nightwoodeditions.com

TYPOGRAPHY & DESIGN: Carleton Wilson
COVER IMAGES: freeimages.com; Wikimedia Commons

BRITISH COLUMBIA
ARTS COUNCIL
An agency of the Province of British Columbia

Canada Council   Conseil des arts
for the Arts   du Canada

Nightwood Editions acknowledges financial support from the
Government of Canada through the Canada Book Fund and
the Canada Council for the Arts, and from the Province of
British Columbia through the British Columbia Arts Council
and the Book Publisher's Tax Credit.

This book has been produced on 100% post-consumer recycled,
ancient-forest-free paper, processed chlorine-free and printed with
vegetable-based dyes.

Printed and bound in Canada.

CIP data available from Library and Archives Canada.

ISBN 978-0-88971-314-7

For Dennis and Anita Thran

CONTENTS

III—RIVER

I

CARAPACE

YOURS, AL

Documentary footage.
You are in the same spot
where I am sitting
inside of your house
right now. Surprise!
You are reading
a poem. Same sofa,
same blue curtain
behind your head. You are
projected from my laptop screen,
where I used to get updates
from a cousin who worked
in the Arctic on one of those
breakers. Areas of
the North you wrote about
are gone. Icebergs
unlike mirrors
pass by. What is it
doing to my face
to be here in your life
in my life?

*

What is it doing to my face
to be here in your life
in my life?
The blue Smith Corona
on a stool-top perch
in a sca of morning
light. Your tin
of silver bullets. A man
has just opened fire
on Parliament Hill. An MP
is whispering over the airwaves
to Anna Maria Tremonti
from under a desk.
They haven't killed
the perpetrator yet.
The present moment is long
and full of fear.
What would you make of this,
Al?

*

What would you make
of this long day
from swamp land
bush land
up since six a.m.
with child?
We have read,
fed, listened in to the fear
and now walk the rural
roads. Late fall,
by now you'd already be
in Mexico, in Greece.
I can see my breath
and the breath of horses
you've never met
on the corner of Whitney
and Gibson Rd.
Ex-racer, black.
The matted one's name
is Jack. I sit out front
beside the stroller,
beside the foundational
stones of your burned-down
garage. On the remains
of the wall
leaf-shadow waves
snapdragon waves
and it looks like
a dinosaur's tail.

*

A softer tail,
your feathered
dream catcher
on the writing-room wall.
Here's your horsehead
shoehorn. Your ancient
empty can of
Kounty Kist Corn.

Shall I go on
making an itemized list
of the things on your desk?
How much
starlight
lakelap
cavepaint

would you need to pile onto
the present age
to convince your reader
time might melt
into some pure form
or swim downstream
or simply change?

*

Your change tin.
Your shortwave.
Your seashell.
Your pinecone.
Your bird's nest.
Your paintbrush.

Whole kernel corn.
Sweet as a Kiss
—Honest as Mother Earth!

*

Honest as Mother Earth?

The pipes are frozen.
The lake is freezing over.

Go outside.
Listen to dogs howl.

How do we live
without power?

How does anyone live
without power?

Beginning tonight,
with the soluble snow.

ONLY THE BARNS

Only the barns seem able to make any sense of this country.
Only the wind-worn wood, which folds over the empty spaces
where utility once creaked towards passion and cruelty.

The barns don't do impressions of stones or their maternal groves
of trees. They travel their own ways into the field and the field
and the field and the field and the symmetry. A little bit off

from the roads and their carnage of snake guts and frog meat.
A ways back from the glimmering hubcaps and plastic
princess kiddie pools. A long drive to the nearest major city.

Invite the Minister of the Environment into a barn, any barn,
to answer hard questions about policy. Invite the petroleum
    ad-writers
into another, to wax on about repurposed tailings ponds water.

And after the last words have been uttered in the dusty, federal air
and the guests have been ushered back into the sunlight, broadcast
the insides of the barns. Only the barns. Their public is listening.

POEM WITH TOO MANY TURTLES

It has been raining all morning, but to hell with it, four of us
travel the slick roads and POW! the sun appears during a scenic
coastal stretch. I wade into the lake with my daughter affixed
to my chest. From a distance, I must look like her shell.
S. splashes through the water towards our group
with an actual turtle in her hands—ornate orange-spackled
hood and decorative markings. We *oooo* and she lets it back
into the lake. On the drive back we spot two different turtle-
crossing signs, and then two different rocks that I mistake
for turtles, and I slow down on account of the warnings.
In the spirit of the signs and the sun we grind the day down
to a lurch. Decide to visit Purdy's grave. There's a pot
of flowers and, yes, a little stone turtle that someone has left
on the headstone. I pull the camera out for a group photo,
but our friend is shy, angles his head away, curls his eyes up into
his paperboy cap. (Come to think of it, Purdy himself
looks hunched like a turtle in all the photos.) At the cabin
we drink beer under the canopy of trees, and later I lower
my child's bald head into the play yard, read from *Les rêves*:
Papa tortue rêve sous sa carapace, then give a quick kiss to S.
before she burrows under the thick duvet. I catch the news
and recoil at the stories of people disappearing: women,
children, journalists. Then have my own dream under the moon
in its case of black cloud: there are three poachers with duffel bags
full of contraband shells. They live down the road in an old
        silver trailer.

LOCAL WEIRDOS

I do not actually believe that the cows are snickering
in the nearby fields, even though I have left drops
of my own blood on the A-frame floor
after chipping frozen patties with a knife
and putting the blade into my own hand.
S. careens the car down Highway 62, baby blowing
raspberries in the back, tractors and tourists slow
on the road, and me in the front seat bleating—
one quarter in pain and the rest in self-reproach
for having jabbed metal into the fine-tuned machine
of the day: sections for working, sections for caring
for child: balance and poise and elaborate dance
gone to cud with one slip of the handle. S., sure
hand on the wheel, says go easy on yourself,
as though editing the melodrama out of the poem
I am not composing. We don't crash. There's no
lineup at the hospital, where the doctor, steady
as Sunday service, works the thread and needle, saying,
"Knew there was a poet in our midst, but to us
he was just another one of the local weirdos."
The nature of cows seems gentler on the calm
drive back. Go easy. I'm all stitched up. Glad
of the baby, of S., of Al , of cows. Of the doctor too.
Time thaws us all. I judge men as harshly as he does.

BEDROCK

Snow falls. My friend is in the middle
of a particularly long and degrading chapter
in his story. Snow falls. I listen.
There is an understanding between us:

I'll let him go on for as long as he needs to,
and he'll grant me a certain amount of amnesia.
Snow falls. It's one of the conditions we can

still agree on. Not like the wheat or the trees
or the sky. He talks of the lake like the lake was
today. Like he could afford the beer and the gas.

My friend is myself. I've inherited this.
We've been talking the same way for eons.

THREE TREES

The aspen, the maple and the willow gathered one morning for coffee.
"I don't know how to properly measure my limited hours
against the excess of love that I feel for my fellow aspen,"
lamented the aspen. "There's just this constant sense of having
let down my own kind." "My husband is unreachable,"
said the maple. "He is too many tiny, stacked logs.
A part of him is always away in some fire or the other."
"The plight of the ant makes me weep," said the willow.
"And the plight of the grass. And the nasty things humans
will sometimes call one another as they glide by in canoes."
Their conversation sounded like a day would sound in its entirety.
They pressed their foreheads together at night and otherwise
did not touch, though something was surely going on
under the soil, among roots that only the most agile bugs could see.
How many days passed like that before our family arrived?
How many years? Morning. A pot of hot coffee.
At the edge of the lake, three trees.

EARLY RISING AT ROBLIN LAKE

One could mistake the angular arm
of the plastic lawn chair
for the heron's neck. This before coffee,

just after the alarm
of our infant's voice. She who
rises according to the needs

of her belly, and speaks thanks
to the aureole of her mother's
nipple, in the pre-verbal gurgling

onto which we project, like wind
on the lake, the score
of our earthly belonging. I'm

to toast my bread and brew my pot
and turn the space heaters on
in preparation to greet her, to lease

her mother a couple more hours
of sleep. And so the heron—
majestic, lithe—outside the kitchen window

is a distraction. Curved
like the cane of an elder or the back
of a lover. Its neck a kind of toggle

as the lake becomes a grey screen
on which the past and the future
play out in an endless loop

to the changes of weather. It does me
no good to break the heron's neck,
to mimic more infamous patterns

of speech, or to cede the day
to the bird's own self-strange bidding.
Instead I go into the sleep-haze

of our house, pick our child up
from the bed and proceed
as though the heron were watching

through the window
onto the human shore—before light
and the sobering beans

do their thing—
and I come clear
to the fact that he isn't.

A DRONE'S-EYE VIEW OF ROBLIN LAKE

The film crew's in the living room drinking my coffee.
The drone's on the front deck where apparently Purdy
sometimes rode a stationary bike, blaring bagpipe
music from the record player. Some days he'd swim
out from the point through the weed-heavy waters.
In the buff. All of this hearsay from gossipy neighbours.
Trick is, in the air, avoid casting a shadow. The shadow
reveals the shot's done by a drone. Better to believe
in a bird, in the free-floating viewer's eye, or the poet-
hero soaring fists-out through the air like a knocked-out
Lebowski. Purdy wrote lovingly about his '48 Pontiac,
combines, the knickknacks inside his shed,
so it stands to reason that he'd love this drone
out on his deck, and offer the technicians grape wine
instead of this coffee. So a drunk dive down through
autumn leaves, through the stripped-wood roof, through
the squirrels' nests, to crash like the man at the church
who once hammered the sky. Big guy. Big, big voice.

PS—Dug my stay here,
but I will shake him off me.

II
MAYOR

MAYOR SMALL TIME

We stormed the city that was only a hamper and blanket.
We burned down a pound of ground beef on the stove.
We mounted our horses. Our horses were broomsticks.
We published our presto real-time manifesto.
Our bedbugs marauded on the backs of mice.
The drum was a tin of Café Bustelo.
The guitar strings were plucked from the drain of the sink.
We were small time, and getting smaller.
We crashed the iron gates. Our horses were toothpicks.
A jar of mango chutney smashed to the ground.
We got down on our knees with damp terry cloths.
We were as naïve and hopeful as toddlers
waddling out across the room that for us was the Earth.

CORRUPT CENTO

So many seas.

The water pulls
at our bright cynicism,
at love's struggle,
at the dead

on buttered toast.
Only the stone's light
spreads itself.
Only the sun's
trained parakeet,
Gea, sings

of bullets,
stars,

of the dark places
wherein our friends
are hidden

in narrow beds
over the cliffs.

MAYOR FAITH

That was the time we were full of faith.
People shook our hands in the streets
and wished us well. Kids rang the bells
on their bikes. Birds preached in the trees.
Whatever they said, we believed them.

MAYOR SNOW

The mayor's accountant was as humourless
as a glass of snow.

A glass of snow was on the lawn.

The tongues of the deer
are the tongues of the gods
according to local legend.

The deer, growing brave,
dipped their little tongues into the glass
while the mayor's accountant
holidayed with his shame.

He put a gun to his mouth
as the sun shone in Boca Raton.

Snowfall continued at home.
The mayor's spiel was the same.

RUN WITH THE CREEPS

At a shop window, he stares at a custom-made leather shoe. It glows like the hull of a conquistador's ship. Starting price: five grand. Would it leave a trail of slug-slime wherever he walked? Would hummingbirds fly from dress-print jacarandas to feast on the ghastly sweetness of that trail? Would the walk turn into a run—past the stately brick buildings, past projects, past the firepits where kids roast plastic dollar-store Halloween masks of cats and pigs, past the last brittle-boned streetlamp, and out onto the boiled-peach-skin surface of the river? Would it float? Would it chart a course backward through history? Would it stomp on each image in the kingdom of images? He lingers there at the window and wonders, knowing it's creepy to linger, maybe even to wonder. Then a sewer rat slides out from inside of the shoe like a magician's rabbit, and stares at him, and doesn't seem afraid.

MAYOR AMONG TITLES

found

Those things we treasure:
a sovereign idea, a life
on the fringe. Fragile freedoms.

Citizens of the world,
peeking through the keyhole
towards a just society.

The good fight. The enduring
vision touched by Tommy
and the river of history

contesting Clio's craft.
Banking on deception,
a deal's undone. If you're in my way,

I'm walking yesterday's roads
as others see us:
man of myth and fool of Christ.

Reasoning otherwise
by loving our own,
Canada's founding debates

the Canadian founding.
Strange things:
our glory and grief, tar sands,

sweet promises and sailor's hope.
Ocean to ocean,
the grey owl belling the cat.

MAYOR CONFETTI

(*Thanksgiving Parade*)

A classic mistake by a few rookie shredders:

Now Chad's SIN on the shopkeeper's shoulder,

Brit's date of birth on the vendor's umbrella,

Ethel's savings deposit on Ethan's shirt collar.

*

It's what floats upon floats in the light in November.

A disco ball breaks at the end of the fever.

An agent accepts a quick toke from his neighbour.

A motorcade spawns at the mouth of the river.

MAYOR PEACEFUL PROTEST

The cathedral roof is lipstick red and next
to a lily-pad expanse of glass
on pillars of cement. High-rise, beige,
juts out to the left, snaps back. See

how that white wall spindrifts into it,
replete with long, rectangular windows
like pieces of wave-battered wood?

Picture a dishwasher's top rack.
Toddler twins. All of their bright,
bright plastic doohickeys and blocks.

Can't shake the deafening noise overhead?
Helicopters keep a panicked clock.
And this dispatch, funded by all fronts,
is in the business of displacing difficulties.

THERE IS CONDENSATION BEADING FROM THE INSATIABLE MACHINES OF CORPORATE AND GOVERNMENT SURVEILLANCE

Cameras are out as soon as the weather warms.
Helmed by two careful cartographers

in company-issued threads. No doubt,
their precision is bread on the table

and what's done with their replicas of the city—
every pebble in the sidewalk, every mannequin's

synthetic, eyeless face—is a decision made
by the men and women behind reflective glass

in towers where it's still possible—down here,
looking up from the street—to confuse

the reflection of a single cloud
with some random thing about someone dear

that only a handful
of confidantes knows.

MAYOR ERASURE

Got word there'll be
no comment on

some film
we've never seen,

filmed somewhere
we've never been,

on a night we don't film there.

RUN WITH THE CREEPS

A streak of hair gel and sweat shines on his pillowcase. She lies unclothed in the dark beside him, moving like mist off the lake at the family cottage. Middle of the night, deep in the city's engine; what unaccountable atrocities are taking place? What meat cleavers lie in the tulip patches? What knives are propped blade-down in the compost bins? What if the misspelled words on alley walls are clues to crimes? 'Creep' spelled with a K, with seven eeeeeees. No one's born a creep, he thinks; it comes upon you with the stealth of silverfish, until all of the self-help books on the table look like concert T-shirts eaten by bleach or time. He would like to wake her now, but she has already left through the window, is already smoke. The gel and sweat has settled into a thin crust on the pillowcase. He breaks it apart, sweeps up the flakes. He will have to walk across the street for coffee. Call the council. He will have to call his wife. A bouquet of jet fuel perfumes the valley. The cut bank's infected with purple loosestrife.

MAYOR ARK

Lo!
One more animal enters the city.

A brief encounter
three-quarters into the film:
brakes slam
and the headlights shine
in the animal's eyes,
and the animal enters
the man.

A percentage of each viewer's mind
is freighted with such scenes.

With shivers that fissure
aquarium glass,
that haunt the yard
behind the central plot.

Even the rat
we spotted pages back
still means and means and means.

MAYOR DRONE

found

Imagine what Louis XIV could've accomplished at Versailles
   if he'd had one.
There's been a lot of discussion. I was given a drone. I loaded
   the appropriate app

and went down to the beach. The view I was "seeing." The
   photos were stunning.
There's been a lot of discussion. I was given a drone.

So much has been done in the past without drones. No high
   hill to stand on,
no helicopter to fly in. I was given a drone. Imagine what
   Louis XIV

could've accomplished at Versailles if he'd had one. I went
   down to the beach.
The view I was "seeing." Unacceptable commotion on the
   beach. I was given a drone.

The immense and elegant redesign I could not even begin to
   fathom. A tremendous amount
of speculation. I was given a drone. The view I was "seeing"
   with the help of my drone:

my properties, a hike in the mountains, a day at the beach.
   No high hill to stand on.
Unacceptable commotion. I don't have all of the answers. I
   went down to the beach. I was given a drone.

MAYOR ACTION FIGURE

(with accessories)

Hat a bad tipper. Briefs are long-winded.
Collar folds down like the eyes of a dog.
Coat needs a paintjob. Wristwatch
is under surveillance. Twenty-five years
schlepping through this one-horse dolls'
house, clipping and clopping those wingtips.
Wallet's an open windowlet. Last pair
of slacks are on their last legs. Belt's
cinched tight as a bow tied by lawyers
the former associates drove
directly into the contact lenses
that are being sold separately, now,
to whomever spots one
under the lowboy's bottom (cash) drawer.

MAYOR PARABLE

If a tree falls
across the middle of a downtown street, everyone hears it.
The real estate agent trying to sell the suddenly de-foliaged
walk-up hears it. The woman whose sedan sports a toupee of
branches hears it. Her insurance agent hears it. When a tree
falls

across the middle of a downtown street, there are the sounds
of the saws, of her car backing up, of the wood-chipping
truck; then a few random conversations around the stump
as people go about their business. If a tree falls

across the middle of a downtown street, a crew will come
around later to inspect the site. Maybe one of the inspectors
will mistakenly leave a live radio next to the stump, and the
disembodied voices of municipal workers will live for a while
on the air for everyone to hear:

for grocers on smoke breaks, for a woman out walking her
son, for a man who wanders the streets answering his other,
more private voices. Do you hear them? he asks. Yes, she says.
And they'll stand for a while just listening to the air, to work
on other streets, to the tree

where it fell.
And this hearing's essential to structural health.

MAYOR ESTATE

Winter on the mountain.

Pink gums of dogs
between the gates
of bare trees.

Visible now
are the snow-
filled pools
that border the backs
of an alien wealth.

III
RIVER

THE SILENCE OF SMALL TOWNS

I'm afraid of the silence of small towns,
of the silent gears grinding through small-town traffic
and the clatter of cups in the empty cafes.

And riverstones—especially riverstones.

And the bridge—the tiny, inaudible bridge
that one must cross. Bridge over the river that runs

through the centres of small towns—

through the centre of the silence of small towns.

RIVERSTONE

I'd breathe in noxious emissions for hours
on the sidewalk beside the big brass doors
under the awning of the plush boutique hotel.

I worked with Mohammed, who always had glowing words
for his daughters. With Jeff, who represented us
to the union, and had a preternatural understanding

of each dupe attempted by management. Dave,
with whom I drank most nights. My shifts were
from three to eleven, so the street would go through

a costume change or two over the course of a day,
through two or three desires. It was my duty to be
accommodating. If you needed your car parked,

I'd park your car. Needed help with your luggage,
I'd carry your luggage. There were things I wouldn't do,
of course, but those are better left unsaid, and besides

were only asked intermittently: some strangeness
in the air, in a glass, in the junior suites. But the faces
on those notes would never ever change: Wilfrid Laurier,

John A. Macdonald, Queen Elizabeth II.
If we were lucky, William Lyon Mackenzie King
or even Robert Borden, god forbid. Exhaust caused

pain in my sinuses. So did smokes on the loading
dock bridge after bringing the Benzes around.
Chit-chat with coworkers folded the hours.

Back out front I felt at home with those for whom
the shakedown was a thrill. Concocting parking scams
during gala events, tipping off cops for a fee,

sending waves of guests to an Italian place we knew
we could eat at for free after punching-out.
With Mohammed, who sent half his earnings home

to Mumbai. Jeff, who played in a band whose name
was a misspelled muscle car. Dave, who knew
where the booze flowed after the bars closed down.

I celebrate it all: sore back, hangovers, heavy stuff;
even the noxious emissions, which made sunsets stunning.
I do it to try to redeem an idea of myself. Though I failed

night after night to do anything good. To squirrel away
some of that dough for a later date. To dream. Best-case
scenario on that street was a sudden summer shower:

the beautiful women of Yorkville made even more visible,
the musicians outside the conservatory of music
protecting violas and tubas with every free part of their bodies,

children splashing and running in circles while tired
commuters pushed past, shielding their heads
with the news. The air felt cleaner after, breathable,

and the street took on the glow of the lobby's marble.
The museum was still building its Lee-Chin Crystal.
And even I knew this could not be sustained.

THE PARTICULAR MELON

Walid was making a film about a particular
honeydew melon. *This* melon, he said,
pointing to the table littered with back issues

of *The Economist*, a BlackBerry Pearl, assorted
suspiciously pigmented utensils, and the melon,
which lolled back and forth as their knees hit the table.

Why *this* melon? Frank asked. He was curious.
He was over-caffeinated. And why a film? Surely
it has something to do with the fruit trade

outside Lanzhou, the nefarious laws imposed
upon the disenfranchised? No, Walid said.
Let me stop you right there. I mean *this*

particular melon; which bears the fruit of a
singular summer. With its case like the skull
of a human being. Handled as quickly

by the hands of the pickers and transporters
as by the hands of the grocers, then cradled home
up two flights of stairs by my mother, lighting

the back end of her recurring shoulder injury;
she, the first female underground boxer
out of Pennsylvania in the 1960s. Wait, Frank said.

So this is a film about boxing? Barriers?
A blow-by-blow account of your mother's rise
to the rings of New York City? The melon

as a symbol of motherly love, a warrior's prowess?
The flesh of the fruit a symbol of memory,
of the toll the blows took over the years. How,

having forgotten the details of her past, she remains
a scooped-out shell of her former self, until the seed
of familial love and artistic direction is planted by

your camera lens, and the world sees her as she was,
anew? Wow, Walid said. You've had a lot of coffee.
Please let me finish, Frank said. I want to understand *this*

particular melon, and perhaps a clerk, brunette,
late teens, holding it above her head and calling
for a price check while the rest of the line

grows anxious and impatient. Holding it steadily
while your mother looks on, admiring her strength
and thinking, perhaps, that she is seeing the torch

being passed from one generation of boxers
to the next, as sentimental and distractedly triumphant
a moment as she has ever known in the ring,

spitting blood into her bucket, while the fat cats
in the front row spill vodka tonics on their leather shoes.
Then, Walid said, we will funnel the chords of a song

through the air between her missing teeth.
Something distinct, Frank said. Yes, Walid said,
something fresh off the heels of the blues.

ELPENOR FOR YUSEF

When he broke, he broke
like an oak box
full of castanets tossed
into a frozen river.
He broke like a stuntman
through the plate glass
of Odysseus's conscience.
Broke like a breakdancer
shattering his right knee
while doing a backflip
under the Liberty Bell.
Broke like the promise
he swore he'd never break.
Like the teen who leapt
out of *Another Gravity*.
Broke like the brakes
on an underground train
hurtling at breakneck speed
into Rubén Darío Station.
Broke like bits of glass
strewn over the steps
on a Sunday morning.
Broke as all hell. *Keen*
for the cool night
air broken. Roused
by soldiers marching,
when Elpenor broke
he broke the spirits
of all mortal men.

MAGNOLIAS

Loving flowers, and lingering long,
I know you wish *my* eyes weren't drawn
to every empty beer can in the park,
every unfurled tire tongue on the trail,
every condom wrapper on the pond.

I understand. Of course, you also see
the traffic cone tangled in that tree?

I'll climb up there and bring it down.
I'll make it make a trumpet sound.

You're like the Tony Montana of spring pollens!

I know you don't get that reference.

But there's your bemused, indefatigable face
glaring at me from the stupid magnolias.

THEY WILL TAKE MY ISLAND

I love a plow more than anything else on a farm.
    —Arshile Gorky

Say in the painting, soldiers storm the field,
cradling their mothers' sex
under their arms like gourds.
Say Freud, trying to flee the scene,

trips over the still-hot coals
in Picasso's *Guernica,*
and reignites an age's fires.
Then Gorky's mother's limbs

do start to look like his.
And then his mother's name
does start to sound the same as his
when it's called out over the trembling field

for however long one person's death can last,
which, including blockades in the aftermath,
is far too long a time. Say all of that's there
for a while in the painting, and then

it isn't there. And being certain that
it was conceived on Crooked Run Farm
in Virginia, some thirty years on—
say that I love the name of the farm

more than anything else on the farm;
that I'd bring that up to make this mine.

OAK BAY BASKETBALL, 2006

after the painting by Tim Gardner

There's nobody playing against you.
Nobody watching you go to the hole.

You've perfected your left hook,
can dunk with two hands.

Morning through the elm trees casts
a series of shadows onto the road.

Morning through the elm trees casts
a net on the lawn and your brother's not there.

Your mechanics are sound.
There's nobody watching.

This is the man
that you'd want him to know.

INSOMNIA ON ITS WAY TO THE COMOX VALLEY

Black string tied to the door handle.
Milk in glass jars, on the steps.
The dog lost, scavenging somewhere
in the day's first light. How early
is too early to call out once? I whisper
the name of the grandfather who rests
in a field while some of his children
haul stones. While my father, ten, at work
in the barn, beheads the evening's meal.

It's too early to call the carcass clean.
Removing the black string from
the door, I speak Sleep's name
in the voice of the dog. Eat through an idea

of the day. Call out once, and no doubt
I'll follow with the second call,
the third—and then I'll be out on the trail
covered in fleas, covered in burrs,
holding the end of the string in my mouth,
forgetting my name. Commuters en route

compare my face to the one on the yellowing ad.
Look at your collar. Where is your home?
I could make it out to the final stop,
fly in a plane, cross the strait
by boat, make a slow trot down the road.

Good boy, says my father in the voice
of a child. The rooster calls. The leash in the grass
is the grass itself, is the dirt itself, is sleep
as the children have tried to sleep
among the unspoken details and ruins.

TROUT

Consider the daughter.

As I'm already prone
to wild bouts of sentiment,
she'll probably finish me. As in look:

a trout leaps from the grocery list
while she totters so carefully over the lip
where our turn-of-the century floor dips south

that the bread crumbs between my fingertips
break out again into rounds of applause.

Here are the spears of asparagus.
The scales of all symbols are sequined with cold.

Consider the fish, the wayworn floor.

See how the dials in my eyes start to wave.
My love is a radio tuned to a law.

OBIT

She says the moon has got so low tonight
that it's polishing the rail.
—Jason Molina

Moon's a Jason Molina
of grief tonight,
sad as the look in
Seymour Hoffman's eyes
from the year's list of obits.
The perpetual, pouring
condolence note.
The grief muscle always alert
and working through grief.
A crow is the collar
of a funeral suit.
A flock like the black lace
of a funeral shroud.
Real grief and also
the practice of grief.
Tom Hanks is going to die.
Tom Hanks is going to die
just as the mountain
and the aspen will die.
And there are the Quincy
Robert Scarlett Ferrell
Garfunkels of future grief
polishing rails alongside
the Joan Rivers of grief
that run to the cold, dark sea.

MARGINALIA

Works to have your own set of coded symbols,
a shorthand easily deciphered, later,

when you begin to uncoil your own thoughts.
But I love the scribblers who can't help themselves:

full sentences, double underlines for emphasis.
Sontag couldn't, and so a green grew all over

the stones. Or picture Bolaño as a young graffiti artist.
Or take my wife's old copy of *The Grey Islands*,

which I'm reading right now. There are so many
scrawls in the margins that reading this book

is like moving my hands through her hair
before I arrive on a shore where the protagonist flirts

with the dangerous idea that he needs no one else.

THE PRIVILEGE OF SMALL TOWNS

At the limits of my vocabulary
for another's pain, I must pack
my bags.

And when, later, I find myself ringing
the bell on a desk late at night
in a small town—

legs weak with the day's heat,
and nobody answering;
I have to consider

that I am probably the keeper of this inn.

SEVERS TALKING

I chose this book because the author is a yellow contemporary poet. The Clearing Paper is his third book. The book is divided into three different SEVERED: The distance devoured by wolves, blank notebook, and ultimately, Self Portrait at the clearing. The shape of all the poems is "prose poem" are poems without jumping lines. The first severs address a second person voice ("you"), which is likely the poet myself "you approach." I also said that because he quotes the poet Fernando Pessoa Portuguese famous at the beginning of the book. Fernando Pessoa wrote as many people. The "You" of these poems is "insoluble face." Many poems speak with a mental disease that manifests as nature pictures and images of the body. The second severs talking to a third person plural "we." The voice of these poems is already a lonely voice, but he speaks of our collective diseases such as wars, destroy the surrounding, etc. In the last severs he addressed himself as "I." Images that recur are elementary images like snow, fire, mouth, etc. The whole book is very dark, a little violent, but I love his desire to speak in a voice "clear as had live" without history, "light as a bird ember found in the hollow of the hand, finally mine."

NOTES

I

All the poems in this section were written during a three-month stay at Al and Eurithe Purdy's A-frame in Ameliasburgh, Ontario. D.G. Jones, in his essay "Al Purdy's Contemporary Pastoral," argues that Purdy's poetry is an illustration of "how to live without power."

II

I accidentally included in "Mayor Small Time" an approximation of a famous line from Mark Strand's poem "My Life." Upon realizing this, I immediately appealed to some folks at city hall to have it altered. But the mayor, who (somewhat surprisingly) owns numerous autographed editions of Strand's early works, wouldn't change it.

"Corrupt Cento" is written using the lines of fifteen different poets, then erasing all but a few words from them. I failed to record what all of the poems were, but Wisława Szymborska, Fernando Pessoa and Raúl Zurita are responsible for essential turns.

"Mayor Among Titles" is comprised entirely of full titles from the office library of a political science professor at the University of New Brunswick.

"Mayor Drone" is comprised entirely of text from Martha Stewart's *Time Magazine* article "Why I Love My Drone" (July 29, 2014).

III

"Elpenor for Yusef" is written after Yusef Komunyakaa's poem "You and I Are Disappearing."

"They Will Take My Island" is after a painting of the same name by Arshile Gorky.

"SEVERs Talking" is a failed book report on Mario Brassard's *Le livre clairière*, written in my own French while studying at a provincial language school in Montreal. It was run back through Google Translate, and then re-tinkered with for "clarity" of phrasing.

ACKNOWLEDGEMENTS

Thanks to the editors of the following print and online publications, where earlier versions of many of these poems first appeared:

The Walrus, Matrix Magazine, Taddle Creek, Riddle Fence, EVENT, This Magazine, The Fiddlehead, Bodega (USA), *Congeries* (USA), *Cordite* (Australia), *Hazlitt, They Will Take My Island, Concrete & River, I Saw it at the Movies* (Guernica), *Tag: Canadian Poets at Play* (Oolichan Books) and *The Best Canadian Poetry 2014* (Tightrope Books).

Both of the "Run with the Creeps" poems were originally written and recorded for D-Sisive's hip-hop album *Run with the Creeps* (Urbnet, 2011). Thanks to Derek Christoff.

This book was written with the generous support of the Canada Council for the Arts and the Al Purdy A-frame Association. My thanks to the organizers and facilitators of these programs, and to the people who fund them.

Thanks to Jeffrey Gustavson and Sue Sinclair for insightful and helpful edits. Thanks to the friends who looked at individual poems. Thanks to Silas White, Carleton Wilson and everyone else at Nightwood Editions.

All my love to Sue and to Abigail.

ABOUT THE AUTHOR

Nick Thran's previous collection of poems, *Earworm*, won the Trillium Book Award for Poetry. His first collection, *Every Inadequate Name,* was a finalist for the Gerald Lampert Memorial Award. Born in Prince George, British Columbia, Nick has lived and worked in various towns and cities across the country, most recently in Montreal. He works as a poetry editor for Brick Books and is the 2015–2016 Canadian Writer-in-Residence at the University of Calgary.

PHOTO: PETER SINCLAIR